Wheels, wings and water

Buses

Chris Oxlade

www.raintreepublishers.co.uk

Visit our website to find out more information about Raintree books.

To order:
- ☎ Phone 44 (0) 1865 888112
- 📄 Send a fax to 44 (0) 1865 314091
- 💻 Visit the Raintree Bookshop at **www.raintreepublishers.co.uk** to browse our catalogue and order online.

First published in Great Britain by Raintree,
Halley Court, Jordan Hill, Oxford OX2 8EJ,
part of Harcourt Education.
Raintree is a registered trademark of Harcourt
Education Ltd.

© Harcourt Education Ltd 2003
First published in paperback in 2004
The moral right of the proprietor has
been asserted.

Editorial: Charlotte Guillain and Isabel Thomas
Design: Sue Emerson (HL-US) and Joanna Sapwell
(www.tipani.co.uk)
Picture Research: Maria Joannou and
Su Alexander
Production: Lorraine Hicks

Originated by Dot Gradations
Printed and bound in China by South China
Printing Company

ISBN 1 844 21373 0 (hardback)
07 06 05 04 03
10 9 8 7 6 5 4 3 2 1

ISBN 1 844 21383 8 (paperback)
08 07 06 05 04
10 9 8 7 6 5 4 3 2 1

British Library Cataloguing in Publication Data
Oxlade, Chris
Buses. – (Wheels, wings and water)
1.Buses – Juvenile literature
I.Title
388.3'4233

Acknowledgements
The publishers would like to thank the following for
permission to reproduce photographs: Collections/
Peter Wright, **14**; Collections/ Ray Roberts, **19**;
Collections/ VI, **6**; London Transport Museum, **4**;
Trip/ B Turner, **17**; Trip/ Derick Thomas, **10** Trip/ H
Rogers, **7, 9, 11, 12, 13, 16, 18, 21, 22**; Trip/ P
Treanor, **15**; Tudor Photography, **8, 20**;
Tudor Shooting, **5**.

Cover photograph reproduced with permission of
Collections/ VI

Every effort has been made to contact copyright
holders of any material reproduced in this book. Any
omissions will be rectified in subsequent printings if
notice is given to the publishers.

Contents

Some words are shown in bold, **like this**.
They are explained in the glossary on page 23.

What is a bus?

A bus is a **vehicle** that carries lots of people.

This bus is carrying people around a city.

These children are going to school by bus.

People who ride in a bus are called passengers.

What kinds of bus are there?

This is a double-decker bus.
It has two decks.

Some buses only have one deck.

Coaches carry people on long journeys.

There is a big space for **luggage** underneath the seats.

What do bus wheels do?

Buses have big wheels.

The wheels let the bus roll along the road.

tyre

Each wheel has a fat **tyre** to stop the bus from slipping on the road.

The tyres make the bus ride less bumpy.

What makes a bus go?

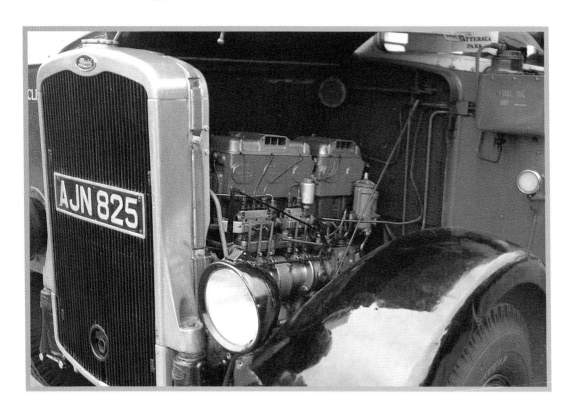

A bus has an **engine** that makes its wheels turn round.

When the wheels turn round, the bus moves along the road.

An engine needs **fuel** to make
it work.

The fuel goes into the fuel tank.

What does a bus driver do?

A bus driver steers the bus left and right.

She also makes it start and stop.

The bus driver collects the **fare** from every passenger.

Where do buses go?

Most buses work in towns and cities.

Each bus follows a route through the streets.

Some busy roads have a bus lane.

Cars are not allowed in the
bus lane.

Where do people get on and off?

People get on and off the bus at a bus stop.

Passengers ring the bell when they want to get off the bus.

Buses start their journeys at a bus station.

These buses are waiting to start their journeys.

What bus runs on rails?

A tram is a bus that runs on rails.

It is like a train that drives on the road.

tramlines

The rails for a tram are called **tramlines**.

Tramlines are buried in the road.

Who looks after buses?

Sometimes buses get dirty.

The bus station has a special bus wash to clean dirty buses.

Some parts of a bus wear out.

A mechanic replaces the old parts with new ones.

Bus map

seat

mirror

route sign

wheel

driver

Glossary

engine
machine that makes a vehicle move by making the wheels turn round

fare
money that a person pays to travel on a bus

fuel
liquid or gas that burns in an engine to make energy

luggage
the things that a person takes with them on a journey

tramlines
metal bars on the ground for the wheels of a tram to go on

tyre
rubber strip on the outside of a wheel

vehicle
machine that carries people or things from place to place

Index

Contents

Mosquitoes

Mosquitoes are tiny flies. Some are so tiny, they are difficult to see.

You need a magnifying glass to see a mosquito clearly.

Different mosquitoes

Gnats and midges belong to the same family as mosquitoes.

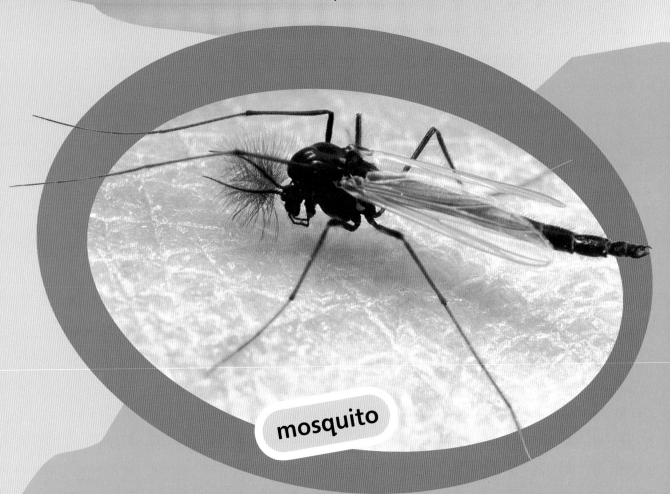

mosquito

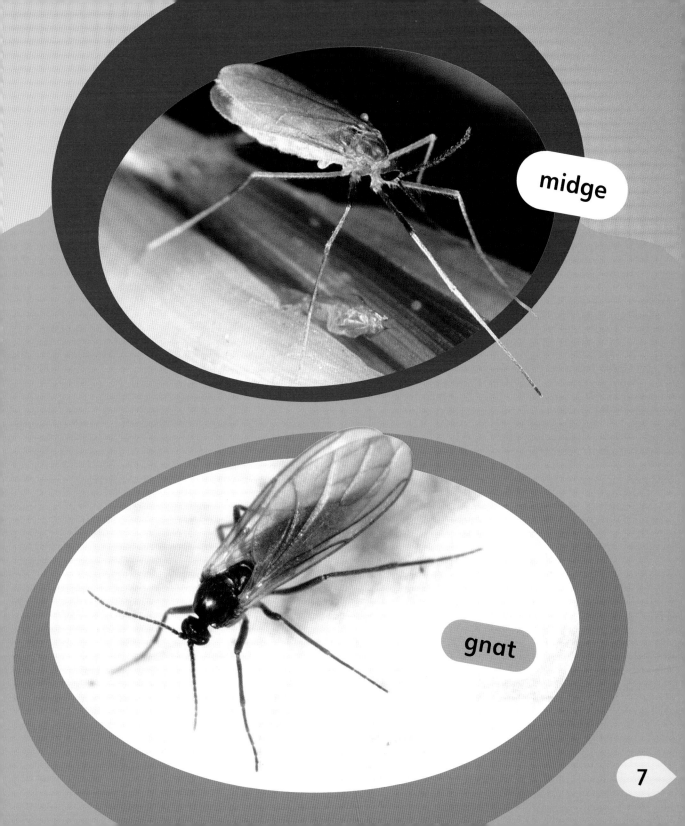

midge

gnat

7

Looking for mosquitoes

Mosquitoes live near ponds and ditches.

You might
see them on
a summer
evening.

9

A mosquito's body

Mosquitoes are insects. Their bodies have three parts.

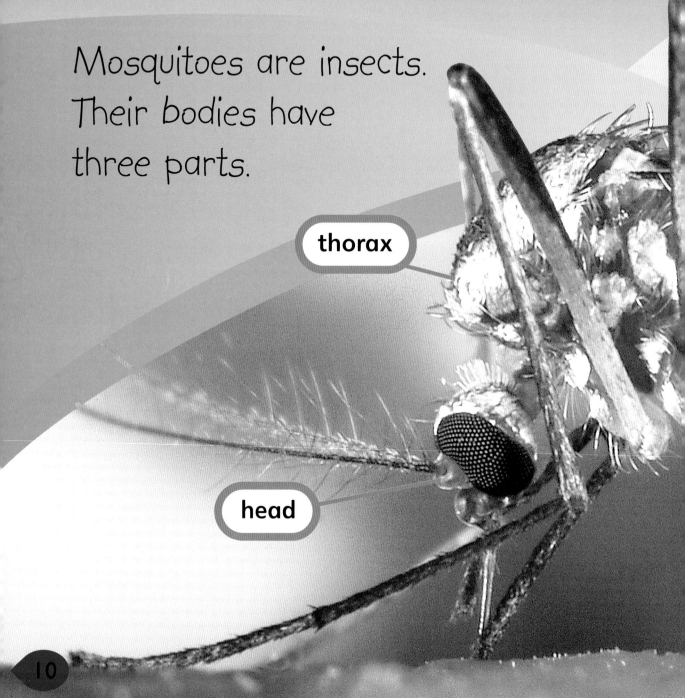

thorax

head

They have six long legs.
How many can you count?

abdomen

A mosquito's head

A mosquito has very **sharp** mouthparts for piercing and sucking.

Their feather-like antennae are used for touching and smelling.

antennae

Mosquito noises

Mosquitoes make a whining sound as they fly around.

EEEEEEEEEEEeeeeeeeeeee!

14

Zzzzzzzzzzzz!

Their wings beat so fast that they make a noise.

15

A mosquito's eggs

A female mosquito lays hundreds of eggs on still water.

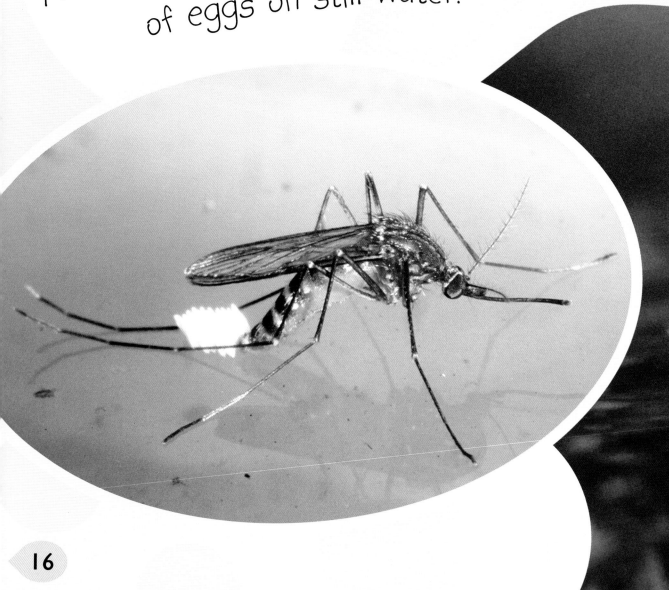

She lays them in groups that *float* together.

17

Growing and changing

The egg changes into a larva that **wriggles** in the water.

Finally, the adult mosquito waits for its wings to dry. Then it can fly away.

Food for mosquitoes

Male mosquitoes eat nectar, which they suck from flowers.

Females eat blood, which they suck from animals.

Dangerous mosquitoes

When mosquitoes suck blood from people they can spread diseases.

Ouch!

There are creams
to help if you
are bitten.

Index

Notes for adults

This series supports the young child's exploration of their learning environment and their knowledge and understanding of their world. The four books when used together will enable comparison of similarities and differences to be made. (N.B. Many of the photographs in **Creepy Creatures** show the creatures much larger than life size. The first spread of each title shows the creature at approximately its real life size.)

The following Early Learning Goals are relevant to the series:
• Find out about, and identify, some features of living things, objects, and events that they observe
• Ask questions about why things happen and how things work
• Observe, find out about, and identify features in the place they live and the natural world
• Find out about their local environment and talk about those features they like and dislike.

The books will help the child extend their vocabulary, as they will hear new words. Since words are used in context in the book this should enable the young child gradually to incorporate them into their own vocabulary. Some of the words that may be new to them in **Mosquitoes** are *thorax, abdomen, mouthparts, antennae, larva, nectar* and *diseases*.

The following additional information may be of interest:

Mosquitoes are tiny and delicate, but they are one of the most dangerous blood-sucking insects. In some tropical countries, female mosquitoes can spread diseases such as malaria, and they are the cause of millions of deaths every year. Mosquitoes feed mostly at dusk or during the night. Female mosquitoes need a meal of blood because this provides proteins necessary for the development of their eggs. Some mosquito breeding grounds can be treated with insecticides, and draining and filling of ponds and ditches is sometimes carried out as a more permanent solution. However, these methods of control may cause pollution and other environmental damage.

Follow-up activities

Children might like to follow up what they have learned about mosquitoes by making their own observations in parks and gardens. Develop ideas and understanding by discussing any features they find interesting, and encourage children to record their observations and ideas in drawings, paintings, or writing.